Drawing and Painting
Landscapes

Drawing and Painting

Landscapes

ALBANY WISEMAN

COLLINS & BROWN

First published in Great Britain in 2004 by
Collins & Brown Ltd
The Chrysalis Building
Bramley Road
London W10 6SP

An imprint of **Chrysalis** Books Group

Project manager: Nicola Hodgson
Editor: Roger Bristow
Designer: Jon Morgan

Distributed in the United States and Canada by Sterling Publisher Co.
387 Park Avenue South, New York, NY 10016, USA

10 9 8 7 6 5 4 3 2 1

British Library Cataloguing-in-Publication Data:
A catalogue record for this title is available from the British Library.

ISBN 1-84340-081-2 (hb)

Reproduced by Classicscan
Printed in Singapore by Kyodo Printing

Contents

Chapter 1

Materials and methods

The history of landscape art goes back to early Chinese painting, long before it was introduced into medieval western art as a backdrop to religious imagery. It was not, however, until the eighteenth century that artists such as Turner and Constable began treating the landscape as a subject in its own right, working directly from life in the open air.

Since then, the popularity of landscape painting has grown enormously and artists of all levels, both amateur and professional, take great pleasure in capturing the beauty of the landscape.

This book is an invaluable introduction to drawing and painting a wide variety of landscapes and includes skies, mountains, trees, rivers and lakes as well as the seasons and the time of day.

This first chapter looks at the range of materials available to the landscape artist and how best to use a wide variety of different media, from pencils, pastels and pen and ink to gouache, acrylic and, of course, watercolour.

Paper

COLOURED SUPPORTS
This simple watercolour was painted on a 'Turner Blue' handmade paper. When working on coloured papers in watercolour the only way to achieve whites is with the use of body colour, as here.

COMPARISON OF MARKS MADE BY DIFFERENT
MATERIALS ON CARTRIDGE PAPER

Reed pen

Charcoal pencil

Fountain pen

Graphite pencil

Paper, sometimes called 'the support', is the primary material for artists of all skills and will accept all the media included in this book. It comes in a variety of weights, textures and colours. It is essential, therefore, to know which papers are best suited to both your ability and your chosen technique.

For preliminary studies, brown wrapping paper and sugar paper provide inexpensive and interesting surfaces on which to work. Plain white cartridge paper, which comes in a variety of weights and qualities, is another economical surface which accepts a wide variety of media.

For pencil, pastel and Conté, the fine Ingres papers with their 'laid' lines (faint patterns made during the manufacturing process) give interesting textural effects. These come in a wide range of colours.

Artists using watercolours and wishing to use more specialized papers have three main surfaces to choose from; smooth (or hot pressed), medium rough (sometimes called NOT), and rough. These papers are readily available. Others that are more expensive include handmade papers such as Turner Blue and Green, named after the eighteenth-century artist.

The density or weight of paper is measured in grams per square metre (GSM). When painting in watercolours or using diluted ink washes on lighter papers (up to 140 GSM) it is advisable to stretch the paper prior to using (see page 26).

Portuguese boats
Papers with a rough surface allow the artist to experiment with a variety of textures and wash techniques when making watercolour sketches such as this marine study.

Mediterranean landscape
A simple study of trees and hills made on an Arches heavy, rough paper, an excellent if somewhat expensive surface. Good quality papers such as this, though, do not need stretching prior to use.

Pencils – tone and grades

Graphite pencils, commonly known as lead pencils, are the basic tools for drawing. It is essential, however, to keep pencils sharp when in use. This is a simple task but a vital one. Use a scalpel or sharp knife for this. Fine sandpaper is useful for refining a pencil point. Each pencil grade will give its own tonal range from the hard H pencils to the softer Bs. 'Chisel' point pencils, which give broader marks, are also available.

Paper surfaces and textures will significantly influence the pencil's mark. Experiment with a variety using different hardnesses of pencil to find the combination that suits you best.

When drawing with a pencil think of it as an extension to the arm with the shoulder as the pivotal point.

SCULPTURAL PLANTS
I used a 4B pencil to render this drawing of teasels in a landscape. Its rich black line suited the plants' complex and sculptural seedheads.

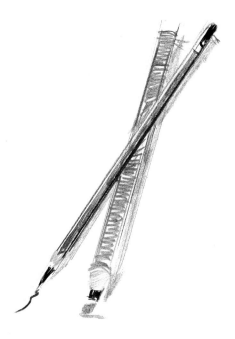

VARYING THE TONES

Try doing pencil drawings using a range of grades. The cross-hatched sky and detail in the middle distance in this drawing were made with a 4B pencil, whereas the bolder marks in the foreground were made using a carpenter's 'chisel' pencil. Drawn on a smooth paper.

THE WHOLE RANGE

In this study   a wide variety of pencil grades was used, from an 8H in the sky to an 8B in the foreground. The rough surface of the watercolour paper, as used here, gives texture even to the hardest of the pencil grades.

Coloured pencils

Coloured pencils, whether watersoluble or not, are a useful addition to your drawing materials for use outdoors. There are many makes and qualities of pencils available, either in sets or individually. Coloured pencils respond better to smoother papers as the colours blend more easily than on rougher surfaces.

Watersoluble pencils should not be regarded as a substitute for watercolours, but they are easily carried, and are useful for making colour notes and sketches as well as finished drawings in their own right.

When using watersoluble pencils blend the colours with a wet brush to simulate a watercolour wash. The pencil colours become stronger with the addition of water so experiment on a spare piece of paper first.

Conté coloured pencils are made of a more chalky material, and are closer to pastels.

Areas of fine colour detail

Soft was

PENCIL AND WASH
The initial drawing of this grain store in eastern England was made with a graphite pencil. Coloured detail was added with water-soluble pencils, some areas of which were washed with water to achieve a watercolour effect. The hard, smooth surface of the paper allows for fine pencil detail and soft wash effects.

RURAL STUDY

This drawing of an old windmill in southern England was made with various grades of graphite pencil with colour added using non-soluble coloured pencils. It was drawn on a smooth, hot-pressed paper, a support well suited for fine detail.

BLACK AND GREEN

An architectural study in fine black pencil with the addition of a limited range of coloured pencils used to add a range of hues, mostly green, to the vegetation.

Coloured pencils (continued)

LIMITED COLOUR

It is not necessary to use a wide range of colours. In this study of a French chateau most of the drawing was done with graphite pencils with a limited use of coloured pencils giving a pleasing, monochromatic effect.

BEACH SCENE

A simple study made with coloured pencils on a medium watercolour paper – a pleasing surface for pencil rendering.

QUICK SKETCHES

Don't feel obliged to render every detail in a pencil drawing whether in black and white, or in colour. This speedy sketch used a mix of coloured pencils and graphite and concentrated on capturing the essential elements of the scene.

Straight edges where a mask has been used

Masking with paper

In this loose, coloured pencil study of a broad panorama the vigorous qualities of the pencil shading were contrasted with the straight edges of some of the drawn areas. These were achieved by using the edge of a piece of scrap paper as a mask.

Focal point

Soft coloured pencil drawing was used to describe this tunnel of trees – a common sight in rural France. The small splash of contrasting colour at the end of the tunnel draws the eye into the picture.

Pastels

Working with pastels (sometimes known as 'painting') can be a rewardingly direct technique for image making. They are made from powdered pigment bound with gum Arabic. This mixture is moulded into sticks which harden as they dry. Pastels are readily available in hard or soft versions as well as more waxy, oil-based versions.

Soft pastels are made in a wide variety of colours and can be blended using a 'torchon' (a compressed paper stick) or by making 'broken' strokes – laying one colour against another to create a lively image. Hard pastels come in a smaller range of colours but, unlike soft pastels, can be sharpened. Pastel pencils are also sold in a limited range but can be sharpened and, being enclosed in wood, are cleaner to use.

The more oleaginous oil pastels produce different marks to conventional ones and have the advantage that you can thin them with turpentine in the same way that you can with watersoluble coloured pencils and water.

Pastels take well to a variety of paper surfaces. Ingres papers, having a sympathetic texture, are popular with pastel users but there are cheaper alternatives including brown wrapping and sugar papers.

All finished pastel paintings should be fixed to prevent smudging. But, beware, use sparingly - too much fixative will darken the image. When fixing hold the can about 46 cm (18") away from the image. Fixative is not eco-friendly and it is not advisable to use it in a confined space.

WINTER SHADES

The delicate shades of pastels are particularly suited to winter studies, as in these two studies. Both were drawn on to tinted Ingres paper, a particularly suitable surface for pastel works. They were drawn very directly with little or no rubbing to soften tones. A detail of this is shown, left.

Direct pastel marks blending together

Pastels (continued)

Broken colour
effect on pebbles

Broad, horizontal
strokes on path

VARYING THE TECHNIQUE

A number of pastel drawing techniques were used in this rendition of a French lighthouse.   The foreground pebbles were drawn using a number of hues to create a 'broken colour' effect. A similar method was employed in the sky, but with a more limited colour range and a greater dependence on hatching.

FREE RENDITION

Lively pastel drawings can be made using a free and vigorous approach as here, top right. Works such as this can be used as reference for later, more detailed drawings.

SMOOTH SURFACE

Study of Portuguese fishing boats made using Sennelier oil pastels, on to white inexpensive mounting board. This brand has a very oily, soft quality, and the colour range is wide. If this brand is not available, substitute with a similar oily pastel. These pastels are very strongly pigmented, and can be diluted with mineral spirits or turpentine, blended with a brush or used directly on to the support.

Pen and ink

Drawing with a pen is a positive and direct way of making marks. Specialist pens are not necessary, a good fountain pen will provide you with a useful means of recording detail and texture and, with the right type of paper, give a loose, fluid line.

Dip pens, when used with a flexible nib, can produce both thick and thin lines. With their need for bottled ink, however, they are less convenient for outdoor use than fountain pens. Other traditional pens, such as quill and reed, both available from good art suppliers, give a line quality not easily achievable with other pens.

Modern pens, such fibre tips and technical pens, are easily carried but generally produce an insensitive and mechanical line.

Both watersoluble and waterproof inks are available; the watersoluble allows you to work into a pen drawing with a wet brush to create interesting wash effects.

The kind of paper you choose will influence the quality of your pen drawing. For example, a soft Ingres paper, with its 'laid' lines, will spread the ink marks slightly whereas a hard paper, like Schöllenshammer, gives a clean, fine line. This paper also allows the artist to erase wrongly drawn lines with a scalpel. Other smooth papers, such as hot pressed watercolour paper, are ideal for more detailed studies.

Deep shadow areas rendered in near blacks

Shadow areas drawn in angled cross-hatching

GRAPHIC RENDITION
The linear qualities of this clapboard house in Cincinnati, USA, were described with a technical pen. Although these can often give hard and uncompromising effects I felt that the contrasting patterns of shadows and wooden construction were best suited to the hard line of such implements.

CONTRASTING
TECHNIQUES
 Two sketches clearly demonstrating the wide variety of effects achieved by using a sepia, fibre-tip pen (top) and a range of coloured inks applied with a dip pen (below).

FOUNTAIN PEN AND MASKING FLUID

This drawing of rural houses in the north of England was made using a fountain pen on a large sheet of paper, 41 x 51 cm (16" x 20"), allowing a broad use of techniques. The grasses in the foreground were initially drawn with masking fluid (see pages 32–35), allowing them to read as white line when they had been overlaid with brushed ink work and the masking fluid removed.

cal suggestions
of brick or stone
often enough to
convey the
character of a
building's fabric

Bolder line work
in the foreground
accentuates the
sense of depth in
the drawings

SOFT LINE EFFECTS

Although this Mediterranean scene was drawn with a fountain pen, usually resulting in a strong, firm line, it was made on soft white Ingres paper which caused the ink line to soften and 'bleed' a little, rather like drawing on blotting paper.

HARD LINE EFFECTS

This drawing was made on an extremely hard paper, giving a sharply defined line. It was softened by smudging the initial ink drawing with a wet finger.

Pen and ink (continued)

URBAN LANDSCAPE

A black and white sketch of an American townscape made with a fountain pen loaded with black ink. Carrying a fountain pen is a convenient way of having a readily-accessible drawing implement when a likely scene presents itself.

FINE DETAIL

A dip pen used on a smooth surface, such as this cartridge paper, allows for fine line work and detailing.

URBAN CLUTTER

A sketch done in a Corsican town with a fountain pen on Ingres paper. Adding the visual paraphernalia of an urban scene, such as cars and street signs, will help convey the sense of place.

INK AND WASH

When using watersoluble ink, as in this study, easily achievable wash effects can be made by working into the drawing with a brush and water.

'LEFT' SPACES

When drawing with a pen don't feel obliged to cover the whole of the paper. The viewer's eye will fill in blank areas such as the expanse of road.

PATTERN AND DETAIL

Pens are particularly useful for depicting scenes with a variety of patterns. The busy drawing of the stones and plants in the foreground of this drawing lead the viewer's eye towards the distant church.

THICK AND THIN

When sketching with a fountain pen use the front of the nib for bold, foreground marks and the back for rendering distant detail, as shown to good effect in this Scottish landscape.

Painting materials

There are a number of kinds of paint available to the artist today including watercolour, gouache, acrylics (all water based) and oils.

Watercolour is a popular medium for landscape artists, partly because its transparent qualities allow the painter to capture subtle atmospheric effects and nuances of light and shade, but also because of its ease of carrying.

A wide range of colours is not necessary; a good basic palette should include sap green, cerulean, French ultramarine, cadmium red and raw sienna, either in pans or tubes. You will also need three good brushes: a size 10 and a 5, preferably sable, and a large mop. A block of good watercolour paper (see page 8) is essential. The heavier the paper the less likely it is to distort when laying washes.

Gouache is an opaque chalky medium, suited to a toned paper. The relatively new range of acrylic paints, with their ability to be used as thick impasto or thin washes, are fast growing in popularity. Oil painting is not covered in depth in this small book. If used outdoors, the medium will benefit from the use of an Alkyd (some paints come with Alkyd added), which has quick drying properties

If using one of the three water-based media, you will also need a pencil, an eraser and a lightweight drawing board. For working out of doors a sketching stool is also recommended.

PAPER TRIALS
In order to find the paper best suited to your watercolour technique try a number of small experimental sketches on a range of paper scraps. Working in monochrome helps you evaluate these without being distracted by colour mixing.

HOT PRESSED EFFECTS

When working with watercolour on a smooth, hot pressed paper, such as this study of a Mediterranean house, you will notice that washes can dry with a hard edge. This can be used to advantage, especially in architectural studies.

THE QUALITY OF GOUACHE

The use of gouache as a medium in its own right, as opposed to body colour in watercolour painting, gives an opaque finish to the colouring. This can be particularly effective when depicting a Mediterranean subject, as here.

Painting and materials (continued)

A selection of good brushes will be an essential part of your painting materials. Numbers 4 – 10 – 20 will be good for starting out – some 'prolene' synthetics are perfectly acceptable.

Squirrel brushes are available in good art stores and hold a good amount of water and make a good point.

Sables are much more expensive but, look after well, should last many years. Don't leave them in water, and wash them after use.

TONAL VALUES

Practice drawing in tone by limiting your palette to one neutral colour, as below. Paynes grey or burnt sienna work well for such exercises. Even small scale drawings such as this one allow you to evaluate the light and dark areas of a composition prior to beginning a more finished piece.

STRETCHING PAPER

In order to stretch paper to prevent it distorting when used with watercolours you will need a drawing board, larger than the paper to be stretched, and brown gum strip paper about 25 mm (1") thick. Thoroughly wet the paper and remove surplus water with a tissue or sponge. Lay the soaked paper on the board and smooth it flat. Stick the gummed paper all around the edge, half on the paper and half on the board and leave flat to dry.

Don't be afraid to use different media in conjunction with each other. This simple image was made by applying water- and body colour over sanguine pencil drawing, all applied to brown wrapping paper. The finished result captures the warmth of this Mediterranean image.

Body colour used over coloured paper to render paler tones

Watercolour

In spite of its popularity, watercolour painting is a difficult technique to master and errors are hard to correct, unlike with oils and acrylics. Serendipity – 'the faculty of making happy and unexpected discoveries by accident', applies especially to watercolour.

The watercolour process is all about working from light to dark. A newcomer to watercolour should practice a few techniques before venturing into the field. First try laying a wet wash; when dry, add a darker one and observe how to build up colour layers. Try wet-into-wet washes where clear water is laid onto paper and a colour wash painted into it. Observe the variety of different effects that can be achieved with these methods.

Then, using sepia or Paynes grey, try producing monochromatic images to establish lights and darks.

Once you feel comfortable with this, take the three primary colours (red, blue, yellow). Mix them in their various combinations to make mauve (red and blue), green (blue and yellow), and orange (red and yellow). Mixing all three will produce neutral shades of brown. You will be surprised how many colours can be mixed from the primaries. Too many colours in your palette can be very confusing if you are new to the subject.

Watercolour and oil pastel

Wet on dry

Wet-into-wet

MONOCHROMATIC STUDY

A monochrome image made using cobalt blue only. Producing a preliminary, 'thumbnail' sketch in a single colour will make you aware of the tonal values of a picture prior to producing a more finished piece.

IMPRESSIONISTIC RENDITION

Semi-abstract landscapes do not require total accuracy – a sense of place can be more meaningful than photographic realism. A large brush captured the effects of the landscape, working in watercolour, from light (in the distance) to the darker, brighter, foreground details.

Aeroplane's vapour trail drawn by scratching into wash with a sharp blade

Gradated wash changing from ultramarine blue to raw Sienna

Acrylic

Acrylic is a very versatile medium. Not only is it quick drying but it can also be used on a variety of surfaces such as paper and canvas. It can be applied either as a thick impasto or a thin wash. Some colours are opaque, others transparent.

Although acrylics are thinned with water, there are various additives that can be mixed with the paint to give gloss or textural qualities.

Disposable palettes that keep the paint moist during use are handy for acrylics. These have a semi-permeable layer of paper which, when damp, retains the moisture in the colour for a considerable period of time.

Synthetic brushes are perfectly acceptable for use with acrylic paint but ensure that they are thoroughly washed in soapy water after use.

FRENCH OYSTER BEDS

The versatility of acrylic has been exploited in this painting. Thin washes have been used for the sky and water with thicker impasto techniques employed in the foreground and reflections. The smooth board support was prepared by underpainting in a dark brown pigment.

ACRYLIC ON CANVAS

Acrylic can be a speedy alternative to slower drying oil paints. Here a deliberate oil painting effect was achieved by working in opaque paint on canvas prepared with red underpainting.

ACRYLIC ON PAPER

Light red underpainting has again been employed in this broad landscape study on ready-prepared paper. Leaving small areas of the underpainting showing through the study, as seen here, gives a chromatic vibrancy to a work.

Resists and textures

Most of the techniques shown here apply to watercolour but some also can be used in conjunction with gouache and acrylics.

'Resists' are the application of water or paint repellent substances, such as candle wax prior to over-painting. 'Textures' are techniques that are applied to, or combined with, existing painted areas.

Use these techniques with restraint, it is easy to overdo them and give your work a facile appearance.

MASKING FLUID

Art masking fluid is made of a liquidized rubber solution. It is applied before watercolour or ink washes are laid and, when removed, reads as white line. It can also be added to pale washes before applying darker ones to subsequently reveal the paler line work. Wait until it is perfectly dry before working over it with washes and then wait for these to dry before removing by rubbing with a finger. Care should be taken when applying masking fluid with brushes as it can damage them if, after use, they are not carefully washed with warm soapy water. This problem can be avoided by using with a dip pen such as a reed pen (see pages 20–23).

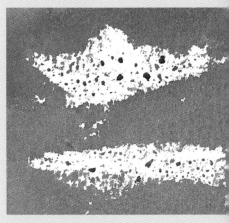

CANDLE WAX

Drawing with candle wax before a wash causes more broken resist textures.

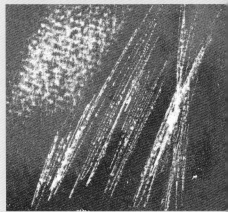

SGRAFFITO

Scratch back into the wash with a sharp pointed blade or fine sandpaper to introuce light line work.

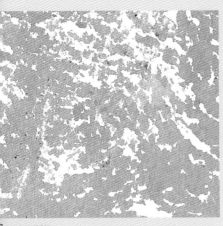

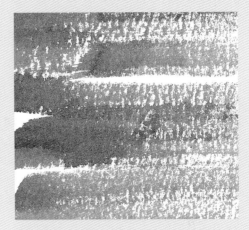

SPONGE WORK
Broken areas of texture are easily produced by applying the paint with an artist's sponge.

DRY BRUSH TECHNIQUE
Interesting linear effects can be made in watercolour by applying with an unwetted brush and dragging the paint on to the paper's surface.

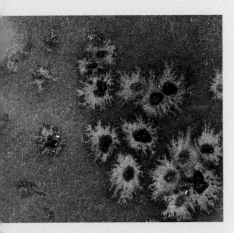

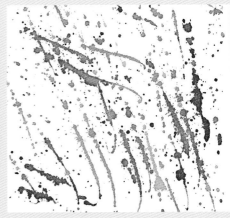

SALT CRYSTALS
Sprinkling sea salt crystals on to wet, dark washes causes unusual snowflake patterns.

SPATTERING
Load an old toothbrush with liquid paint and apply by pointing at the artwork and dragging a small stick or similar it across the bristles towards you. Practice this somewhat random technique before use in order to achieve control.

Resists and textures (continued)

RESTRAINED MASKING TECHNIQUE
Masking fluid is best used sparingly, as in this watercolour painting of a Welsh chapel where it has been applied to the stonework of the building and the nearby tree. Over-reliance on the technique will tend to look mannered and crude.

SAVING WHITES
One of the useful attributes of masking fluid is that it allows clean areas of white to show through watercolour overpainting, as in the two studies below. The alternative, white gouache body colour, can look heavy and dead unless used carefully.

NATURAL EROSION

In order to emulate the effects of ageing on this old headstone on a Scottish moor I applied sea salt to a wet wash. As always, use such techniques sparingly and only where the subject warrants it.

UNUSUAL ROCK FORMATIONS

Although it works in a similar way to masking fluid by resisting overpainting, wax resist gives a quite different result. It is a less precise technique giving a softer, more textured finish, particularly useful for suggesting the textural qualities of these ancient rock formations.

FINE DETAIL

Very fine line detail, such as window glazing bars in these two watercolour drawings below, can often only be achieved by the careful use of masking fluid.

Chapter 2

Elements of the landscape

In representational art, the landscape, more than any of the other classic subject areas, provides the artist with the greatest variety. There is an enormous wealth of different views to choose from including mountains and hills, lakes and rivers, wild forests and cultivated farmland as well as man-made structures in the landscape.

Added to these are the effects of the changing seasons, the diversity of weather conditions and the constantly moving light throughout the day. The most important thing to remember, though, is the sheer pleasure to be gained from working in the landscape. In so doing you will also often be producing mementos of enjoyable times for years to come.

Sketchbooks

There are all shapes and sizes of sketchbooks to suit most needs. They are an ideal first step prior to making more finished paintings. They allow the artist to try out basic art materials economically. Pencils, pen and inks and brushes and paints can all be used in sketchbooks. Some books come with a variety of papers; this can be an effective and economical way of getting to know different colours and surfaces.

The sketchbook has many functions; information gathering and a visual diary as well as a private place to experiment and improve your observational and drawing skills.

Keep all of your sketchbooks, they are a wonderful record of past pleasures.

GOOD QUALITY

Good quality sketchbooks contain paper that doesn't stretch. This watercolour drawing was made in a sketchbook of Arches rough paper.

COLOUR NOTES

Quick sketches, like this one, can be useful as reference for later, more finished work. It is a good idea to make notes on the sketch to indicate what the final colours will be.

COMPOSITIONAL ELEMENTS

Learn to relax with your sketchbook, both in the techniques used and in the composition of your images. Here I began drawing on the left-hand page but allowed the drawing to spread across the fold to give a more panoramic feel.

FIGURE SKETCHES

Market places, such as this one, are especially good locations for quick figure studies. The people going about their business or doing their shopping are unlikely to notice that they are being drawn and will provide natural poses.

Loosening up

Before commencing painting or drawing 'loosening up' exercises can be very beneficial. Athletes loosen up before sporting events to both relax the muscles and help the concentration. A similar exercise by artists will assist in losing inhibitions and learning to relax with whatever drawing or painting tools are being used.

Begin by making random marks on sheets of inexpensive paper – cross hatching, loose rendering or brush marks. Remember, the drawing and painting processes are not only to do with looking hard at the subject but also feeling confident from the start that you are in control of your chosen medium.

Try to work on a large scale; the larger the scale of the piece of work the more freedom you will achieve with the arm and wrist. Most drawing is controlled from the shoulder, particularly when standing at an easel.

COLOURED PENCILS

The free effects of coloured pencil renditioning are particularly useful in loosening up exercises. here areas of tone and shading have quickly been laid down to establish the overall elements of a more finished work.

BLACK GRAPHITE

The rich black qualities of soft graphite pencils lend themselves to strong tonal contrasts in preliminary exercises.

SUNLIT SILHOUETTES

Once again a soft graphite pencil was used to explore the tonal contrast between the sunlit water and the silhouetted islands in the distance.

Linear perspective

The laws of perspective can be daunting and can involve complex theories and principles. However, there are a few simple rules to the basics, which are known as one- and two-point perspective. Once these are understood, the artist will have the means to tackle most problems encountered when perspective is a factor in a drawing or painting. By means of diagrams and simple explanations these basic rules are explained in the following four pages. The main point to remember, however, is that when beginning an exercise in perspective, the first task is to establish the eye level or horizon line.

A CLEAR HORIZON
When viewing the sea from the water's edge, the horizon, unimpeded by undulating terrain, trees or buildings, is easily seen and is level with the viewer's eyeline. The lower the viewer the lower, in consequence, the horizon.

AN OBSCURED HORIZON
Although the horizon in this scene appears to be the tops of the distant hills, the true horizon is, in fact, below them and still level with the viewer's eye level.

A HIGHER VIEWPOINT
When the horizon is viewed from a higher viewpoint, it rises correspondingly.

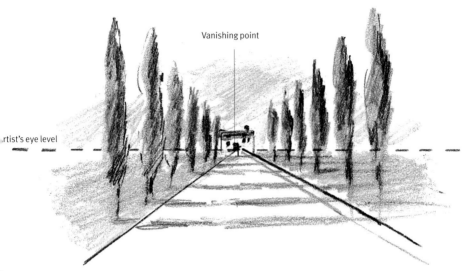

Vanishing point

Artist's eye level

THE VANISHING POINT

The simplest rule in perspective is to imagine parallel lines receding from the viewer. These converge on the horizon at a spot known as the vanishing point.

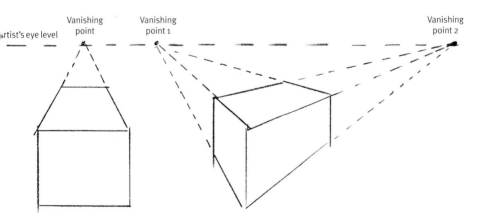

Artist's eye level

Vanishing point

Vanishing point 1

Vanishing point 2

ONE-POINT PERSPECTIVE

If a viewer looks at a rectangular box 'square-on' its parallel sides obey the rule in the diagram (above left) and converge on one vanishing point.

TWO POINT PERSPECTIVE

Seen from an angle (above right) the sides of the box that aren't parallel to each other still converge on the horizon, but at two separate vanishing points.

Linear perspective (continued)

Vanishing point 1

Eye level or horizon line

Vanishing point 2

A BUILDING IN PERSPECTIVE

A building seen from an angle obeys the basic rules of two-point perspective. All of the parallel lines of its structure in any one plane (such as those of doors and windows), recede towards the vanishing point o that plane.

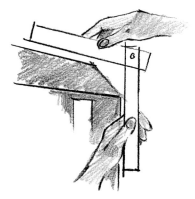

CHECKING THE ANGLES

A simple way of assessing angles in perspective, such as the roof of a building, is to carefully hold a pencil (above left) and align it with the sloping roof. A more accurate method (above right) is to make a simple tool from two pieces of rectilinear card hinged together with a split pin. Position the vertical card against an upright of the building and align the top piece with the angle of the roof. Hold the device firmly in place and transfer the angle to your drawing.

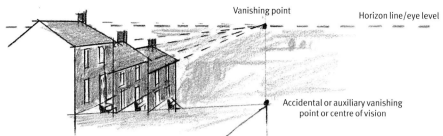

Vanishing point

Horizon line/eye level

Accidental or auxiliary vanishing
point or centre of vision

DOWNHILL VIEW

Seen from above, buildings on a slope still obey the
basic rules of perspective with parallel lines (black)
converging on the true horizon (red) which, owing to
the high viewpoint, is also high. The road itself,
however, converges on a much lower spot known as

the auxiliary vanishing point. This is always directly
beneath the building's vanishing point. A vertical
line joining the two vanishing points defines what is
known as the 'centre of vision'.

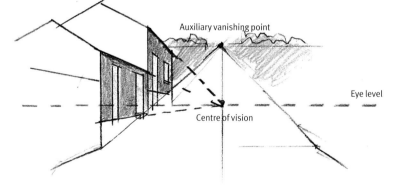

Auxiliary vanishing point

Eye level

Centre of vision

UPHILL VIEW

Seen from below a similar thing occurs but with the
auxiliary vanishing point now much higher than that
of the buildings.

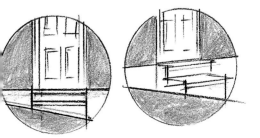

PERSPECTIVE DETAILS

Even small sloping details, such as
steps, follow the same principles. Seen
from the front (left), the steps of the
building are parallel to each other but
not the base. Seen from an angle (right),
the parallel lines converge, but are at
variance with the slope of the road.

Aerial or atmospheric perspective

Aerial perspective is the sense of depth caused by atmospheric effects on the colours and tones of landscape.

The further away the elements of the landscape are the softer and cooler the colours will be, with a preponderance of blues and violets. The middle distance and foreground will be more detailed, textured and stronger. Warmer colours in the foreground will advance and complement the distant blues helping to achieve this sense of recession.

A similar sense of space can be achieved in monochrome with a dark foreground receding into a distant, pale background. This can be produced in pencil drawings by using different grades of pencil, or the use of varying pressure on a soft pencil.

COOL RECESSION

The sense of distance in landscape images will be enhanced by the use of cool colours for the furthest elements. Adding detail to the foreground while keeping the background simple, as here, helps accentuate the impression of depth.

SIMPLE FOREGROUND

Once again, cool blues and violets have been used on the distant hills to convey the sense of recession. Unlike the painting opposite, I have kept the foreground simple and focussed on the distance. This also accentuates depth.

CONTRASTING COLOUR

Horizontal soft blue washes have been laid to emulate the hazy sky and background. The gentle terracotta on the farmhouse roof gives good colour contrast whilst adding a focal point to the painting's composition.

DEPTH IN MONOCHROME

Aerial perspective was suggested in this simple sepia sketch by the use of dark tones in the foreground reducing to pale washes in the distance. Emulate these tonal contrasts, even when working in a range of colours.

Composition ·

These pages show methods of producing visually balanced pictures by using harmony and arrangement – the elements of composition.

The viewer's eye should be led subconsciously into a picture. This can be achieved in a number of ways such as using a strong line or an area of carefully placed rich colour.

A simple compositional technique is to divide a picture into thirds and place an important element at one of the crossover points. Placing major elements at the centre of your composition will usually be uninteresting.

A simple rectangular viewfinder, cut in card (see right), can help isolate areas of landscape and facilitate composition.

When thinking about your composition, never worry about unfilled spaces – these can often add emphasis and interest to the drawn areas.

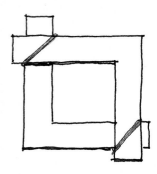

VIEWFINDER
Cut two L-shaped pieces of card, join them at the corners with elastic bands, and move them to suit the shape of the picture and format.

DIVISION OF THIRDS
A pencil sketch drawn using the division of thirds. This shows how the placing of the main elements of the composition have been influenced by this underlying structure. The eye is led naturally towards a point at the end of the road.

Free use of pencil

Figure in distance adds scale and depth

Broad sweep of wash leads the eye towards the distant figure

Vigorous line work in foreground contrasts with fine detail in distance

CONTRAST OF SCALE

Balancing large and small elements in an image creates depth in a picture and adds vitality and dynamism. Here the receding lines of the large trees shadows draw the eye towards the tiny figure in the distance. Watercolour wash over graphite drawing.

The use of 'thirds'

A sketch demonstrating the use of 'thirds' in making a composition – a method much favoured by photographers to achieve an asymmetrical but harmonious composition. The picture area above is divided vertically and horizontally into thirds and a major element of the composition – here the lighthouse – is placed on one of the linear crossovers, making it the focal point of the image.

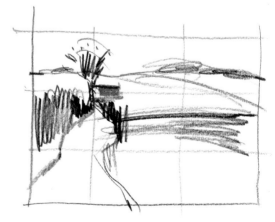

SCALE AND DEPTH

Above I used a receding wall to lead the eye into the picture towards the tiny church tower in the middle distance. The diminishment of scale of the wall's fabric helped accentuate the sense of depth.

LANDSCAPE OR PORTRAIT?

When considering foreground detail, prior to picture making, try making thumbnail sketches in both landscape (left) and portrait (right) formats. Each has its own advantages and qualities, landscape will give a broader, panoramic feel whereas the portrait format is often a useful means for accentuating depth.

Shadows and times of day

When depicting landscapes be aware of the colour and tonal changes caused by the varying light and weather.

A warm sunny day will show many changes from dawn to dusk; in the early morning muted tones, mostly blues, will predominate. Towards midday these will move to warm yellows with hard shadows. In the evening, golden yellows and oranges will be seen with warm colours in shadow areas.

Shadows are best judged by the eye and not theory. You will generally observe that they have a blue/violet cast but will change in tone and colour as well as shape as the sun moves. Make a note of the position of shadows early on in the picture.

Shadows from trees are dappled because of the gaps in the foliage. When projected on to grass the shadow areas will be of a bluer green than the grass itself.

When working in watercolour an ultramarine violet wash with a touch of burnt umber over a raw sienna ground gives a good shadow colour on warm coloured foregrounds.

ISOLATING SHADOW COLOUR
In order to 'isolate' shadow colour from those surrounding it make your hand into a fist with a space between the fingers and palm. Look through this, rather like a telescope, to evaluate the shadow's colour.

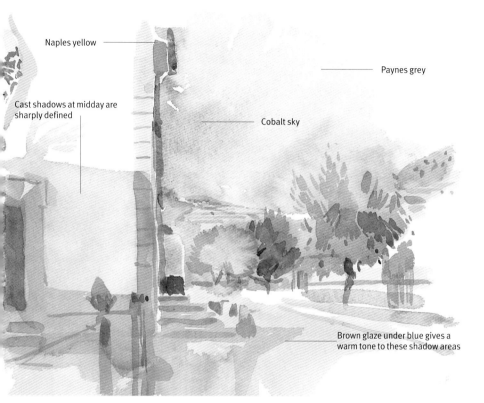

Naples yellow

Paynes grey

Cast shadows at midday are sharply defined

Cobalt sky

Brown glaze under blue gives a warm tone to these shadow areas

SHADOWS AT NOON

A watercolour painting was made at midday in Portugal. This is the time when shadows are at their most intense but always beware of making shadows too dark. Remember the basic rule of watercolour painting – it is always easy to darken a wash but nearly impossible to lighten it. Experiment with colours, both individually and mixed, to find those that best emulate shadow colour.

Shadows and times of day (continued)

Early morning light

The soft qualities of pastels are highly suited to capture the gentle translucent effects of early morning light. In this drawing of a Portuguese river, made just before the sun rose over the distant hill, I knew I had to work quickly as the light at this time of day changes rapidly. Drawn on grey Ingres paper.

Evening light

This quick, watercolour sketch of evening light was made on a heavy Arches watercolour paper. The effect of the misty sun was made by rubbing the underlying wash away with fine sandpaper. Always make sure that the wash is completely dry when doing this and only attempt it on a heavy paper that will accept such treatment.

Misty sun rendered with fine sandpaper

STRONG SUNLIGHT

The sun was high when I began this Spanish
watercolour study. The shadowy colour on the
gateway was achieved with a thin mix of Paynes
grey and cobalt. The warmer foreground, a wet-into-
wet wash, was made with a mixture of raw sienna
and sepia.

Cobalt and cerulean
for the sky

Ultramarine
violet for the
shadows

Light red
on roof

Masking fluid
used for foliage
detail

Wet-into-wet
gradated wash
of sepia and
Naples yellow

Skies

Clear blue skies present fewer problems to the artist than a cloudy ones. Remember, though, the sky overhead is always darker than at the horizon.

Most skies, however, are rarely without some cloud detail. Clouds are simply floating vapour and when rendering them, in whatever media, requires a light touch. The softness of 'wet-into-wet' watercolour techniques (see page 28) is sympathetic to clouds. Charcoal on tinted paper, with added white pencil, is also effective.

Remember that clouds have body and form and are three-dimensional. The laws of perspective apply to cloud formations and their layers get smaller and flatter towards the horizon.

Cumulus (fluffy, white, fair weather clouds) are darker underneath with a hint of yellow on the top. Cirrus, or 'mares tail' clouds are wispy and high, and bring fine weather. They can be successfully rendered with white gouache using a dry brush. Rain clouds (nimbostratus) add drama to a picture.

Practice rendering skies in all media in your sketchbook.

FLUFFY CUMULUS CLOUDS

A quick pastel sketch of a cumulus formation. When drawing such clouds notice how their scale diminishes towards the horizon, as here.

CHARCOAL AND CONTÉ
A combination of charcoal for the darks and white Conté for the lights used on a tinted paper can be particularly effective in rendering cloud studies. Here I chose a dark blue paper to enhance the scene's brooding atmosphere. Fine detail was added with end of a feather dipped in white gouache.

ROLLING CLOUDS
Pastel sketch of a cloudy sky above a low horizon. Sometimes, when there is little visual interest in the landscape itself an interesting picture can be made by concentrating on the sky, as here. Once again, I have made obvious use of the 'division of thirds' (see pages 48–49).

Skies (continued)

WATERCOLOUR EXPERIMENTS

Before attempting to render clouds in watercolour make a series of experimental studies to practise achieving the appropriate qualities and degrees of subtlety.

COLOUR PALETTE

When painting cloud studies in your sketchbook don't be afraid to experiment with different colours. Remember that the sketchbook is a means of experimentation, not a book of finished studies.

EVENING SKY

A simple watercolour study made on a smooth hot-pressed paper. Such papers can cause colour washes to dry with a hard edge. Use this to advantage (see page 25). Experiment with a variety of papers and notice the different effects that can be achieved with washes.

Seasons – autumn and winter

The rich variety of autumn's earth colours – yellow ochre, raw sienna and burnt and raw umber – can be intensely inspiring to the landscape artist. Winter colours, however, bring a change to this palette. Cool colours such as blue, grey and brown predominate.

Cold days are not the best time to paint outdoors but if you can find a warm spot on a sunny day you will notice that the light is sharp, the sun low and shadows long. Winter can also bring snow and mist. Grey winter skies can be dark, especially so when it has snowed. Days like these can be inspirational.

Use a camera for reference on really cold days. but remember, there is no substitute for drawing from nature. Make studies from your window. We often take for granted what is on our doorstep.

CHILLY ISOLATION

An autumnal watercolour study of an isolated chapel in the highlands of Scotland. In order to capture the cold misty colours I mainly limited my palette to burnt umber and olive green with Paynes grey used for the distant hills.

DISTANT DETAIL

A watercolour image of Scottish mountains painted on a cold winter's day. The muted colours of the distant scrub and sandy foreground emphasize the seasonal chill. The ripples in the sand in the near and middle distance lead the eye to the focal point of the picture – the white house below the mountain.

WINTER COLOURS

Pencil and wash sketch of a *pigeonnier* (pigeon house) and chateau in south-west France – typical features of the region. Limiting your palette to cool greys and browns, as here, helps accentuate the chilly atmosphere. If the temperature is very cold, make a quick pencil sketch and add colour notes for later use.

Seasons – autumn and winter (continued)

Bare branches help
accentuate the
wintry feel

VERGLAS
FRÉQUENT

Beware — ice

On really cold winter days it is possible to make
sketches from the warmth of a car. The roadside sign
in the drawing warns against the danger of black ice,
underlying the cold greys and browns of the drawing
with just a touch of red as contrast.

DISTANT SNOW
The wintry atmosphere of this pencil and wash drawing was accentuated by the snow on the distant hills. I used a very soft, 7B graphite pencil to achieve the strong blacks with simple watercolour washes to enhance the sense of atmosphere.

WINTER SHADOWS
A winter sketch made in a London park using pencil and simple watercolour washes. Notice how, in winter, shadows are long and low. Use these winter shadows on trees to emphasize their form, as here.

Seasons – spring and summer

Spring and summer are the seasons when painting out of doors can be a pure joy. In colder climates the bright fresh greens dominate the colours in spring with stronger, darker greens in summer. In warmer climates the spring can bring wonderful colours and carpets of wildflowers – changing in the hot months to ochres and golden browns as the sun bleaches the landscape. Green can be a difficult colour to master when working in watercolour; try adding a little umber or raw sienna to whatever green you are using to soften it. Remember in summer to include a sunshade in your outdoor kit or try to find a place in the shade where the sun won't glare off the white paper.

SPRING SUNSHINE
A bright sunny day in southern France. The patterns in the fields and vineyards were made using a mixture of May green and burnt umber – both useful colours for capturing spring hues. This 'direct' sketch was made with a large brush on heavily textured paper.

Shadows in midsummer are both dense and dark

Warm tonal washes help emphasize the sense of summer heat

SUMMER SHADOWS

Detail from a sketch of trees made in the summer sun. The massed shadows on the trees' foliage emphasizes their form. Green for summer foliage is not an easy colour to achieve. I recommend a mix of varying amounts of ultramarine, raw sienna and lemon yellow, with a little Paynes grey for darker areas.

Seasons – spring and summer (continued)

EARLY SUMMER

A watercolour rendition of a French valley in May.
This study was made in the early morning. In
summer, whenever possible, avoid working towards
the middle of the day. Apart from the personal
discomfort the intensity of the sunlight makes
colours appear pale and washed out.

HIGH SUMMER LANDSCAPE

A sketchbook study
of trees and fields in
midsummer. Filling
a sketchbook with
images like this is not
only useful material for
future work but also a
delightful memento
of pleasurable times.

LUSH FOLIAGE

Looking through a tunnel of trees with strong,
dappled shadows, so reminiscent of summer days.
When working outside with watercolour on
unstretched paper avoiding taking the image to the
edge of the paper, as in this painting, minimizes the
chances of the paper cockling (distorting).

Plants and trees

Tutors in landscape painting classes will inevitably be asked how to paint trees. There are so many species and such a diversity of shapes and sizes that it is a difficult question to answer.

Deciduous trees vary enormously, from the tall elm to the solid shapes of oaks and beech and the delicate form of the silver birch. The seasons see them change from full leaf in summer to their winter 'skeletons' showing their basic structures. Evergreen trees such as conifers vary from tall, spear-shaped varieties to conical forms and low, spreading varieties.

A tree in full leaf has volume, noticeable when light falls from the top or side. One way of learning about how light falls on trees is to light a piece of broccoli from one side and observe how it emulates the effect of light on a tree in full leaf. Acquaint yourself with different forms of leaves and branches and see how they relate to the tree from more distant viewpoints.

Make studies of the bark of different trees. They can be smooth, rough or patterned or even have a distinctive 'peeling' texture such as the plane tree.

SCULPTURAL FORMS

A pencil drawing of pollarded trees in a French village. The trees have been cut back to encourage more shade from foliage. Although these are not their natural shapes trees and shrubs that have been pruned often make interesting forms to draw.

Elm

Poplar

Oak

Cedar

A small apple tree in full leaf

A fallen willow

BASIC TREE SHAPES

Observe how the massing of foliage helps describe the trees' forms.

Elm: tall and full

Poplar: tall and narrow

Oak: low and full

Cedar: layered

TREE STUDIES

Making detailed studies of trees such as this mature plane tree, left, including their bark and foliage gives the artist a fuller understanding of the tree's structure when drawing it from a distance. Fallen trees such as the willow, centre, give an opportunity to study the tree's structure close to.

Inset: study of a *Gingko biloba* leaf.

Plants and trees (continued)

WATERCOLOUR EFFECTS
A watercolour sketch of trees in a French village. The hard edge of a watercolour wash on smooth paper defines the basic overall forms of the trees.

CONTRASTING FORMS
In this pencil study I have contrasted the tall floppy shape of a palm tree in the foreground with the small round shapes of citrus trees in the middle ground and far distance. The trees on the far side of the river have been reduced to mere blobs.

Dark 'negative
shapes'
between the
lighter rendition
of grass stalks

PLANT FORMS

Before making a detailed study of plant forms, such
as this watercolour painting of irises growing in wild
grasses, an understanding of the plant's structure is
gained by making a simple study such as the inset
pencil drawing.

QUICK STUDIES

Use your sketchbook to make quick notes of plants
in the landscape. These can be useful compositional
ideas for later use.

Water and reflections

Painting and drawing inland waters in different locations, in various seasons and changing moods of weather offers exciting challenges to the landscape artist, whether a fast-flowing stream, a slow-flowing river or a still lake with mirror-like reflections.

The movement of water with its attendant waves, ripples and reflections demands concentrated observation from the artist. Notice how a reflection in still water is always slightly darker than its original source. Observe, too, how water seen close to and from above can be transparent but as it recedes its surface becomes much more reflective.

Watercolour, inevitably, with its inherent translucency, is an ideal medium for water studies. Bodycolour can be usefu for adding detail such as ripple effects.

PLACID WATERS
A watercolour sketch of the still waters of a Portuguese river. When water is extremely still it will produce mirror-like images but, beware, the slightest breeze will cause ripples and change reflections to abstract shapes. Decide which you wish to capture before starting your study.

MOVING RIPPLES

A pen and wash study of a nearly dry river bed with water trickling over rocks. Study the way ripples move (see details, right) and watch for repetition so that you can begin to draw them.

Water and reflections (continued)

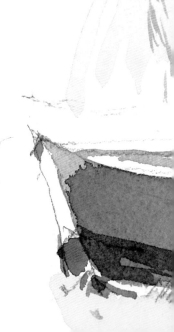

MIRROR IMAGE

A study of an almost perfect mirror-like reflection of terraced vineyards in a Portuguese river. Leaving the almost symmetrical layout of this could have produced a boring composition. I therefore added the right-hand tree to give depth and foreground interest.

REFLECTIONS IN A POND

A watercolour rendition of a still pond as evidenced by the mirror image reflection of the post in the water. When painting or drawing reflections, remember that the reflection is always a few shades darker than its original. Notice how items that are leaning, such as the reeds on the far bank, are transposed when seen upside down in reflection. What few surface ripples there were have been depicted by horizontal brush marks.

Transposed
reflections of
reeds

Reflection of post
is darker than its
source

Ripples
drawn
with
horizontal
brush
marks

Seascapes

The sea has been a favourite subject for artists over many centuries and many famous artists, such as Turner, have produced numerous images of the sea.

It is rare, though, for the sea to be perfectly calm and still and sometimes its dramatic motion can be too agitated for the artist to observe in detail. The camera can record such dramatic moments as reference for future work but remember that this is no substitute for direct observation.

The sea has so many reflections and moods. These, coupled with the textures of sand and pebbles, will give endless inspiration.

BREAKING WAVES
Seas can be notoriously difficult to paint. Do a number of studies until you capture their 'feel'. I find the textural qualities produced by rough paper, such as this, particularly useful for rendering waves.

TIP: A simple way of drawing a rowing boat is to draw a flat figure of eight and join the bow with the shape of the sites of the boat.

MARINE STUDY

Boats – especially those out of water – are complex structures. I wanted to make an oil painting of berthed boats in a harbour and, in preparation for this, produced a number of study sketches, including the one below, which I chose to base the final painting (left) on.

eep brushwork loose and free
hen making sketch studies

Seascapes (continued)

Keep the initial drawing bold and vigorous

WORKING BOATS

A watercolour sketch of beached fishing boats in Portugal. Waterside scenes such as this, with the jumble of unusually shaped boats and the accompanying detritus of planks and flotsam and jetsam offer a wealth of visual opportunity for the landscape artist. Use broad, free wash techniques when working in watercolour to emulate the transparency of the medium.

Mountains and hills

When viewing a range of mountains or hills from a distance they will inevitably appear in shades of mauves and blues (see Aerial Perspective page 46). Seen closer to, the colours will be warmer and the detail sharper.

In winter mountains may be snow-capped. When using watercolour this can be added with body colour or, more simply and effectively, by leaving gaps in the wash where there are areas of snow, allowing the white of the paper to show through.

Keep in the white of the paper for snowy areas. This can either be done by drawing around the areas of snow or drawing white back into the charcoal using an eraser such as a putty rubber. Experiment with this method to see the different results you can achieve.

COLOUR IN LANDSCAPE

Even when depicting a relatively colourful landscape, such as this watercolour study made in the English Peak District, I used as few colours as possible. Here I've used – cadmium, lemon yellow, burnt umber, Hookers green and Paynes grey – a useful combination for landscapes.

Warm foreground tones, giving way to cooler shades in the middle distance

MUTED COLOURS
...study of a remote
...intry valley.
...restricted my
...alette (see
...ages 60–64) to
...mphasize the
...cene's bleakness
...mphasized by the
...ees bending in the
...ind. I added the
...pots of red dye on
...he sheep in order
...o bring a touch of
...olour to the image.

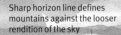

Sharp horizon line defines
mountains against the looser
rendition of the sky

Mountains and hills (continued)

MISTY MOUNTAINS
Mountains, such as these in Scotland, are often
shrouded in mist. When depicting similar scenes
keep your washes light and delicate to give both
atmosphere and depth.

Suggestions of mountain
vegetation are lightly added with
a small brush

Bold foreground detail
accentuates the sense of depth

PORTUGUESE HILLS
Even in sunny climates, the use
of cool colours is essential when
painting distant hills and
mountains (see pages 46–47).
In this study of the Upper Douro
Valley, the distant landscape
was painted in blues and greys.

Figures and animals in landscape

Don't shy away from placing people and animals in your landscapes. Their inclusion will give a sense of scale and vitality to the image. Even a suggestion of a figure can benefit a composition. It can also convey the atmosphere and weather conditions; for instance, a figure's billowing coat on a windy day.

Begin by drawing figures and animals in your sketchbook; these need not be detailed works, quick studies of different poses or in movement that capture the essence of the subject can be just as rewarding as more considered ones.

In rural areas, agricultural animals – cows, sheep and horses are there to record. Their movements and stances can be drawn from every angle. They won't stand still for long but be patient, they will often return to the same position.

A SENSE OF SCALE

Two hikers set off on a wintry day in Scotland. I wanted to include them in this pencil and watercolour sketch in order to give a sense of scale and depth to the building behind them. Including figures in a scene can help accentuate the atmosphere. Here the clothing and the figures' protective stance helps underline the chilliness of the day.

UNUSUAL ELEMENTS
In this sketchbook study of a seaside lighthouse I wanted to demonstrate the size of the tower. The smaller figure walking across the picture plane in the middle distance was able to do this. The second figure, walking towards the viewer, contrasts in scale with the further one, emphasising the feeling of depth within the image. Drawn in pencil with added local colour.

FOREGROUND FIGURE
Without the girl in the foreground this pencil sketch of a Portuguese landscape would have looked flat and bland. The railings, too, using the 'division of thirds', add strength to the composition.

FELLOW ARTISTS
Always keep your sketchbook with you to capture informal figure studies. Even when working in a group you will find your fellow artists offer interesting subjects to draw and paint.

Figures and animals (continued)

TOWNSCAPE INTEREST
Adding a figure to this mainly
architectural study added depth and
foreground interest to this picture.

UNUSUAL PERSPECTIVE
The distorted perspective of this
sloping scene could have been
difficult to interpret without the small
pair of figures seen in the middle
distance and the further, even
smaller figure, framed in the archway.

QUICK RENDITIONS

When making figure or animal studies in the countryside look for figures resting or animals grazing. Try to work quickly. However, there is no guarantee that the pose will be maintained. Cows and horses are largely placid animals and can provide excellent subjects for animal studies.

Buildings in landscape

Like figures, the inclusion of buildings in landscapes always adds scale and balance to a picture. They can also enhance the sense of depth (see Linear Perspective, page 42–45).

As always, practise first in your sketchbook. Compositions often depend on a building or buildings seen close to. Make studies of how tiles overlap, brick patterns and window details. The texture of tiles, brick and stone will add interest to images containing buildings. Understanding these details will also help you when drawing these from a distance.

There is a huge variety of building styles from a simple agricultural structures to complex church architecture. Choose a style to suit your abilities. Every country, too, has its own architectural characteristics. These will help give an authentic sense of location to your work.

PASTEL SKETCH

Pastel can be an ideal medium for making quick sketches of buildings to be turned into more finished studio pieces. The readily-available range of colours and the lack of need for working with water makes pastels an ideal medium for quick sketches without the need for colour notes.

DISTANT LANDSCAPE

When making architectural studies, the inclusion of landscape details gives depth to the image as well as providing the viewer with useful visual information.

MIDDLE DISTANCE COMPOSITION

Placing the image of the building in the middle distance of this watercolour sketch allowed me to include the nearer trees and shrubs in this composition, giving both depth and colour variation

Subtle changes of
roofline define the
building's gentle curve

DISTORTED PERSPECTIVE

Old towns and villages, such as this one in southern
France with its narrow, sloping roads, can offer
difficult perspective challenges to the artist. Look
carefully and analyse the different vanishing points
before beginning such a work.

Industrial and urban landscape

There is often beauty in subjects that are not straightfowardly or obviously picturesque. If you look around you, particularly if you live in an urban environment, you will observe the grandeur in industrial subjects such as powerstations, gas works, dockyards and warehouses. The patterns of cranes and other elements of building sites can also offer exciting possibilities.

Cityscapes, too, are endless subjects for picture-making, whether with modern or old buildings or a juxtaposition of both. A dramatic evening light showing silhouetted buildings can be very inspirational.

The open spaces and parks within our cities provide subjects which combine nature with urban views. The usual can become unusual if you look hard enough.

INDUSTRIAL RIVER SCENE
Rivers in urban regions are wonderful sources for image making. Here, in this deliberately L-shaped composition, I have contrasted the foreground wharves and cranes with the distant shore. Don't afraid to leave so-called blank areas in your work. These can often, as shown, give a sense of space and depth to a painting or drawing.

INDUSTRIAL BUILDINGS, CRANES AND BOATS

Further sketches showing the variety of visual material to be discovered in riverside scenes, from the abstract sculptural qualities of dockside cranes to the interesting shapes of the boats and the towering grandeur of power stations.

Measuring and angles

To aid accuracy with an image it is important to know how to measure and 'frame' a picture and to establish the angles that occur in nature or the slope of a roof. There are a few simple ways of measuring and checking the subjects of your composition.

The human field of vision is limited to 60°. Using a small viewfinder will help to compose a picture in a similarly restricted frame (see Composition on pages 48–51).

The simple 'scissors' shown opposite, are easily made with two pieces of card joined by a split pin – put one side on the vertical then adjust the angle and hold it firm. This can then be checked against your drawing.

Remember that when measuring using a pencil or a brush, it is essential to always hold the implement at a constant, rigid arm's length and with one eye closed. This exercise will be pointless if you do not adhere to these basic rules as you will be comparing inconsistent measurements.

'Sight sizing', another system of measuring, is done by transferring to your paper the measurements of an object exactly as seen.

imple 'scissors' to check angles of perspective.

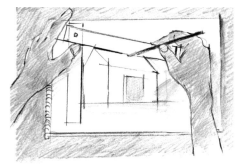

Transferring the angle to your drawing.

hen measuring with a pencil the arm must be
ept straight.

Composing a picture with the use of
a cut-out viewfinder.

QUARING UP

simple grid, made of cotton and card, can be used
scale up a landscape. Hold the grid at a constant
rm's length and, using it as a guide, transfer the
ewed image to paper with similar squares lightly
rawn in pencil.

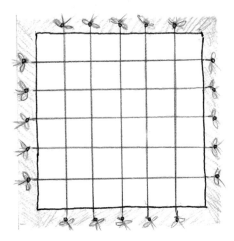

index